How To Be A Good Ally Book 1
500 Ways To Shut Down Hate Speech

LINDA TOLBERT

DEDICATION

To my mother
Janet Tolbert
Who always knew the right thing to say.

CONTENTS

ACKNOWLEDGMENTS

I cannot express enough thanks to Cindy Martin, for your love, friendship, faith, and moral support. My heartfelt thanks to Desmond Cadogan, for your love, wisdom, friendship, and much appreciated feedback on how to make this book better. Some people make choices that change lives. Thank you for being one of them, Nicole Rodriguez (Coach Nicole). You define what a true Soul Sista is. Finally, I would like to express my special thanks of gratitude to Elizabeth Grey, for being someone I could count on to write a wonderful forward for this book, and for being a brilliant, fearless, goddess, who is not afraid to align with her highest self, even when it means abandoning the familiar.

FOREWORD

How do we handle hatred and bigotry?

I am not at all certain I know.

In 2016, I wrote a parody piece about Donald Trump's taxes. Unbeknownst to me, Yahoo news picked it up.

Apparently, Yahoo missed the idea that it was parody. It was presented as straight news.

All of a sudden, the essay had hundreds of comments. I was flabbergasted. As I started to read them, my confusion finally cleared away, and I realized that something I had written had actually become fake news.

The premise of the parody was that I had found Trump's tax returns. I used Donald Trump's own words about Barack Obama's birth certificate, gleaned from his tweets and comments he made, to form the essay. What people were reading entailed Trump's statements about Obama—not mine about his taxes.

This made the feedback particularly hilarious, because Trump supporters reading my piece informed me that I was clearly insane.

They didn't realize they were commenting on the sanity of the president. Then I ran into a few that were suddenly not so funny. It got dark, very quickly.

A few anti-Semitic white supremacists started focusing on me. One of them, incredibly, wrote: I bet her last name is really Grau.

I was terrified. The only thing I knew how to do was exit. I shut down my Twitter account. After the election, I quit writing for a couple of years.

As a woman living in the United States, of course I have experienced misogyny. It's unavoidable. However, I have always been spared other forms of bigotry. My family has been here since 1650. I am a tenth-generation WASP.

I'd never had my safe little perch threatened before. I've always been protected by my privilege. I discovered I really do not like being scared. It shuts me down creatively.

However, I had no idea how to effectively respond to hatred. How do I do it? How do we, collectively, do it?

It's a question I always ask when I stumble upon it, which I do with alarming frequency. Sometimes the hatred is from an anonymous source.

Sometimes it's a politician in Washington.

I grew up in the seventies, and the prevailing sentiment then was to ignore it. If we don't pay hateful people any mind, they will go away. Don't give them the attention they desire.

I think it's safe to say that theory doesn't work. To complicate matters, in the age of the internet, it is impossible to be online and not encounter a misogynist, a racist, or a homophobe. Bigotry is organized. It wants to be in charge.

Almost everyone I know insists that the way to deal with the people propagating hate is to block them. Almost every writer I know has one technique: block and report.

This gnaws at me. I am not at all certain that banishing people helps. They exist. Their poison still radiates, sometimes infecting others. They just move on to another thread.

I am both a cynic and an optimist. I tend to believe that human nature is a complicated mess, and there will always be people driven by hatred.

Concurrently, I cannot believe that there is no way to reach people trapped in that prison. I just haven't possessed the technique with which to effectively handle them.

There's some good news, however. Her name is Linda Tolbert.

When she and I crossed paths online, I had no idea that she would end up being one of the greatest teachers of my lifetime. I just thought she was super cool, and wanted to be her friend.

I got my wish. I also received something else. In the past five years, she has taught me more about myself than almost anyone I have ever known.

One of the wonderful things about watching how Linda deals online is that I can learn by lurking; by simply reading her threads and posts. I don't have to engage to get the benefits.

I have spent five years reading her posts. Sometimes I interact with her, but not often. Usually that's because I am too afraid. Linda is a truth-seeking missile. She obliterates foolishness.

I watch, and learn. What I've found is that in spite of how I think of myself, I am not as unbiased as I wish. Every time I disagree with her, my ego is threatened. I do not want to have racist tendencies. It has never been my intention to have them.

I thought intention was enough. It is not.

Reading how Linda dealt with racism and bigotry teaches me about myself. She helps me become more of a human being; a whole human, not an exclusively self-centered one.

Isn't that the crux of hatred? It makes us less than we are. In James Baldwin's 1949 essay Everyone's Protest Novel, he writes,
Our dehumanization of the Negro then is indivisible from our dehumanization of ourselves: the loss of our own identity is the price we pay for our annulment of his.

Linda insists that people be their best selves.

We've all met people online who wish to explain our racism to us. They share a common characteristic: without fail, they are earnest. Without fail, they inform us that our efforts are lacking. We cannot wait to get away from them.

Linda is not one of these people. She is hilarious--uproariously, boisterously funny. She engages with people with a lightness uncharacteristic of all but the greatest teachers. I think of the Dali Lama, who always looks like he's thinking of a joke he wants to tell; as if he has a secret to this Universe, and that secret is very funny.

Another characteristic she shares with His Holiness, is that even when she's her most acerbic, she comes from a place of Love, with a capitol L.

Her North Star is the truth. It's a compass that always works. She sees the damage hatred causes between people. That she works so relentlessly to alter us, and bring us back to our original state, is a source of hope in my life.

I see her handle situations online which would flummox anyone; especially me. She deftly brings people around to truth, time and time again.

Often, I find myself not understanding what she is doing. There are times she makes me furious.

What counts is that I stick around.

White people like me, especially those of us who grew up believing no bias or racism existed in us, are truly tiresome. Much has been written about white fragility, but it's the truth: we don't want our world shattered. We don't want to give up the privilege we insist doesn't exist.

Linda doesn't let us get away with anything. You just cannot mess with her, or stump her, or confuse her.

She and I have a shared love of our mothers. Once, while describing the origins of Soul Sista #1, her superhero alter-ego, she spoke of her costume with great attention to detail. She told me that she modeled it on clothes her mother wore in the 1970s, when she was, in Linda's words, *In her full power.*

My mother talks to everyone, and I do mean everyone, as if they are a fully-educated, intelligent, forty-year-old adult. I have seen her talk to a mentally disabled person in the same way she speaks to an ambassador.

She couldn't condescend to someone if she tried. She has standards of behavior, and she applies these standards to everyone with whom she crosses paths.

As does Linda. She knocks the wind out of every bigot's sails. She takes away his power, while remaining fully in hers. It occurs to me that this requires enormous discipline. It's so easy to give up on humanity.

It's so easy to say, as the character Rust declares in the first episode of HBO's True Detective, that earth is, *"...a giant gutter in outer space."*

When I think of all the criticism that has come her way—and it has—and how she continues the fight, I am extraordinarily moved.

It's not just for herself, or BIPOC, or women, or a gay child in the Midwest who is being bullied. She fights for us all. She knows we are one.

I am not a person who is fond of adages. They almost never inspire me. With alarming frequency, they make me want to bang my head against the wall. I have a loathing of simple sayings thrown out by people who don't know what else to say.

However, while thinking about how I met Linda Tolbert, one comes to mind so persistently, it deserves to be mentioned: *When the student is ready, the teacher appears.*

We now have her book. Ready or not, to use a phrase of hers, *Class is in session.*

-Elizabeth Grey
July 26, 2020

PREFACE

At age 10, I saw the KKK being interviewed on TV. When one exclaimed, *black people are ugly and stupid*, I thought, *that's not true!*

Afterwards, I asked my mother why he lied. I'll never forget the look on her face as she said, *that's what freedom of speech is.*

She looked angry and heartbroken at the same time. The way all black mothers feel when they realize they can't protect their child from hate.

I understood what Mommy meant, because the term *freedom of speech* speaks for itself, but I was confused as to why the KKK could say *anything* they wanted since *my* mouth always I got me in trouble at school. Then I realized: it only applied to adults.

So, that night I swore an oath to the KKK and anyone who agreed with them. - when I grew up, I'd use my freedom of speech to shut down their lies.

I was too young to understand the connection between the talking sheets and America's apartheid, but I knew words mattered.

Soon after I learned to talk, I started interrupting adult conversations to offer my opinion and give advice.

Grown-ups were amazed I understood what they were talking about. Some looked at me, cocked their heads and concluded, *Janet, there's something odd about your child,* as if I was from *The Twilight Zone.*

I didn't know my advice was sound, until the night I was awakened by banging on the front door.

A friend of Mother's wanted to speak with me urgently. Mommy told her I was sleeping. Before leaving she confided, *Janet, the child was right.*

At age 6 I was in kindergarten. One day a substitute covered for our regular teacher. She was a bully.

While three of us girls, and one boy, were pretending to have tea in the

5

yard, the teacher snapped at him; *boys don't drink tea!*

He was crushed. Sensing his humiliation, I said something to her.

I don't remember my remark, but she became enraged, then grabbed me by my arm and dragged me behind the shed, into *The Twilight Zone*.

Bending down to my height, she put her face close to mine, shook me by the shoulders and whispered harshly, *where are you from? Where are you from? Where are you from?*

Fortunately, another teacher rushed over and yelled, *STOP!* (I guess Rod Sterling was on a break).

Unlike the substitute, the admins and teachers at the nursery already knew I was 'different'.

When a new arrival was distraught, it was my job to comfort and show them around.

I promised them, *we have fun here, and always go home after.* Once they became engrossed in an activity and stopped checking to see if I was there, I returned to my class.

Around the age of 7, I noticed Mommy was a wizard with words.

A regular occurrence at our house can be described in 5 steps: 1. The doorbell rang, and Mommy answered. 2. Someone was upset and wanted to talk to her. 3. They both sat at the kitchen table and Mommy listened. 4. She gave them advice. 5. When they left, their demeanor had changed. They were upbeat and ready to face the world again.

Mommy transformed them with words.

She worked magic over the phone too.

One evening, a couple of weeks before Christmas, Mommy came home upset. She found out the super of our building, who had an attitude problem, fired the maintenance men. In the morning she called the buildings management office and they were rehired. Each one came to the door and thanked her.

A few years later, in middle school, I got some bad news and went home in tears. *Mommy, I don't have enough credits to go to the 7th grade. I'm going to be left behind.*

Mother valued education highly and wasn't very sympathetic. Then I cried, *what hurts the most is my friends are moving on without me.* That got her. She vowed; *I'll take care of it.*

The next day I sat outside the office while Mommy talked to the head of the school. 20 minutes later she came out and declared, *your creativity is important too.*

No one ever got credit for art before, but Mommy reminded the head that my pieces received the most attention on parents' night's and convinced him to give me credits for that. I passed.

Everyone who knew Mommy was impressed by her way with words, but to me it was a superpower, and I wished I had it too.

At 17, I found out I did.

On a rainy night in July I was at a local hangout, an old man's house. He offered me acid and I took it. As it started to take effect a basketball team walked in.

A guy from the neighborhood who liked me was among them. Something inside me screamed, *LEAVE!* On my way to the door I remembered something.

Before going out I stopped at my friend's house to borrow an umbrella. In a beautiful gesture of love and good faith, she loaned me one from her mother's vintage collection.

As I left, she warned, *don't come back without it*, I assured her I wouldn't.

Looking around, I couldn't see it, so I asked, *where's my umbrella?* Someone replied, *in the room.*

When I went to get it, the young man I was weary of followed me, closed the door, and raped me.

Through my tears I could see the others come in and wait their turn. I had to say something.

Suddenly the acid wore off. I stopped crying and focused. Then six words came out of my mouth that made them leave the room. They were, *and you call yourselves my brothers.*

The rapist could have killed me, but my newfound composure made him think he was going to get away with it.

On my way to the precinct with Mommy I was furious, and eternally grateful to whatever took over and got me out of there.

I didn't return with the umbrella. I had something much more valuable - Mother's ability to save the day, or night, with words.

Today, I use Mommy's gift as she did: to encourage, uplift, and speak the truth. Also, I've perfected the art of using the power of words to shut down hate speech. Just as I swore I would to the KKK when I was 10.

INTRODUCTION

According to the United Nations '...*Addressing hate speech does not mean limiting freedom of speech. It means keeping hate speech from escalating into something more dangerous, particularly incitement to discrimination, hostility, and violence, which is prohibited under international law.*

When racism, bigotry, and intolerance go unchecked for centuries, they become the norm and gain momentum. Eventually, they take on a life of their own and live happily in the minds of men and women.

With their systems of oppression in place, they feel safe enough to express themselves as hate speech.

Since words stem from ideas and ideas lead to actions, knowing how to effectively shut down hate speech is the frontline of the battle against hate crimes.

To that end, *How to be a Good Ally Book 1*, teaches you how to spot and stop hate speech against African Americans/Black people, Asian people, Jewish people, LGBTQ people, Mexican people, Muslims, and Tribespeople (the original inhabitants of this land).

How to use this book

As you read, take note of your favorite replies, memorize them, then use them as needed with the authors blessing.

When replying to an online comment, refer to this book and use the best reply for the occasion.

If a reply is met with anger, don't engage in a sparring match. You've done your part by planting the seed of truth. That's enough. As Augustine of Hippo once said,

The truth is like a lion; you don't have to defend it. Let it loose; it will defend itself.

The facts presented in this book can be confirmed by research. If questioned, say, *google it*. Independent research benefits closed minds.

Since the statements and replies may be spoken or written online, quotation marks have been omitted.

Now go forth and fight back in the name of love, truth, and justice for all, no matter their skin color, religion, nationality, sexual preference, or identity.

'Every time the truth is written or spoken; another nail is driven into the coffin of lies.'

- Linda Tolbert

CHAPTER 1
AFRICAN AMERICAN PEOPLE

After 400 years of structural, systematic, institutional discrimination and oppression, racism is arguably one of the greatest crimes ever committed against humanity. The following statements represent white America's almost unanimous indifference to black suffering. They also convey the messages black people have received about themselves for generations from Hollywood, the mainstream media, and society. The replies are formulated to arm black allies with the ammunition required to challenge racism when it opens its mouth to speak or exposes itself on any platform.

I Object to A Black Actor Playing James Bond
(Or Any Black Person Playing A Fictional Character)

- For decades, Hollywood has cast white actors to play black people, Asians, Indians, and Arabs.

- As recently as 2006, in the film 'World Trade Center' a white actor played a black man who was one of the men that helped rescue two Port Authority Police Officers from the rubble of the World Trade Center. Why object to creative casting now?

- There's a long tradition in Hollywood of white actors playing characters who were not white. Why object to creative casting now?

- Actors are playing a part. That's what actors do.

- Good acting doesn't depend on the color of the actor.

- People of all colors can act. That's what matters.

- Equal opportunities should apply to acting roles too.

- Denying someone a role because of the color of their skin is racism. I'm glad Hollywood has evolved past that.

There's so Much Gun Crime in Black Neighborhoods

- White people kill other white people with guns, but the media doesn't call' it 'white on white crime.

- White men top the list of mass murderers in America. They usually do it with guns.

- A white man was caught on camera shooting into a black project. I'm sure he's not the only one.

- Black people can't even allegedly sell loose cigarettes without being strangled to death, who's putting guns in their neighborhoods?

- Obviously, over policing is not effective in black neighborhoods.

- How are those guns getting into overpoliced black neighborhoods? Are they making them in underground tunnels?

- That's weird. Black people are stopped the most by traffic cops. How are they crossing state lines with guns to dump in black neighborhoods?

- We know the CIA was dumping crack in black neighborhoods, who's dumping all those guns?

Black People Are Thugs

- The word 'thug' means a violent person, especially a criminal. White people can also be violent, but they're seldom called 'thugs'.

- White people can be thugs too.

- Violent white people who commit crimes are never called 'thugs', why do you think that is?

- The men on Wall Street who crashed the world economy due to their criminal activity are thugs too.

- Black people are also doctors, musicians, teachers, lawyers, judges, police officers, firemen, EMT's, dentists, opticians, artists, ballet dancers, UPS drivers, store managers, politicians, and homeowners, just like everyone else.

Black People Are Thieves

- Humans sometimes steal. Europeans stole whole continents.

- Black people aren't the only people who steal.

- The white men on Wall Street stole so much money they crashed the world's economy.

- There's a TV show called *American Greed* that features mostly white people who steal.

- Black people had 11 million acres of land stolen from them through fraud, deception, and outright theft, much of it taken in the past 50 years. That's what I call thievery.

- White people have long stolen and benefited from African American culture. Black people don't hold the patent in stealing.

What About Black on Black Crime?

- 85% of white people are killed by other white people. What about white on white crime?

- Good question. Do you think there's something inherently wrong with black people since white people never commit crimes?

- Murderers usually kill the people they're closest too, including white murderers.

- Proximity homicide is the most common among all people. That's why there's so much white on white crime too.

- Most crime shows on TV feature white people.

- What about panda on panda crime?

Black People Commit 54% Of the Crime

- That stat represents the number of arrests. Not the number of people committing crimes. Since the police make up their arrest quotas in black neighborhoods, that makes sense.

- Poverty, poor education, and unemployment caused by 400+ years of racism, are known causes of crime. But the goal is to criminalize black people and return them to slavery in prison, so that stat doesn't surprise me.

- In Alabama, 12 police officers, identified as members of a terrorist hate group, routinely planted drugs, and weapons on innocent black men. I bet those arrests are included in your stat.

- In Florida, during the five-year period from 2008 to 2013, a black man named Earl Sampson was unlawfully stopped-and-frisked, searched, seized, and/or arrested 288 times. Sometimes, he was arrested for trespassing at his own job. With that kind of police activity, we can't trust the crime stats.

- Many innocent black people who are arrested plead guilty, since pleading not guilty would mean remaining in jail, posting bond, meeting trial dates, and spending money they don't have. They're included in the stats you mentioned.

Black People Don't Respect Authority

- Why should they when people in authority usually treat them like they're guilty until proven innocent, like the exonerated Central Park 5 who Donald Trump wanted to execute.

- Respect should be mutual, not one-sided. Many white people in positions of authority are racists who don't respect them.

- This society has done nothing for black people to justify their respect.

- Respecting authority for black people in America means bowing to white supremacy. No sane black person respects their oppression.

- Respect must be earned, not freely given just because someone's in a position of authority.

- Telling black people to respect authority so they don't get killed is like telling women to dress appropriately so they won't get raped.

He Resisted Arrest

- Resisting arrest isn't an admission of guilt. Innocent people don't like being arrested either.

- If you knew you were being arrested because of the color of your skin would you like it?

- Maybe he was guilty, maybe he was innocent. Whatever the case, a cop's job is not to be judge and jury, so he had no right to execute him before trial.

- It's funny how an innocent person can be charged with resisting arrest just because they don't enjoy being arrested.

- Earl Sampson is a black man from Miami Gardens, Florida, who, beginning in 2008, was repeatedly arrested by police for trespassing while at his own place of employment. Some black people have good reason to resist arrest.

He Ran From the Police

- Maybe he didn't want to be one of the countless black men in jail who aren't guilty of anything except being black in America.

- In a racist society, where black lives don't matter, black people have good reason to run from the police.

- With all the innocent black people killed by the police, they have good reason to run from them.

- Whatever his reasons for running, no one fears for their life when someone is running away from them.

- The police kill black men even when they don't run like Philandro Castile, and countless others.

- When innocent black people are arrested, they're told to plead guilty since pleading not guilty would mean remaining in jail, having to post bond, meeting trial dates, and spending money. Maybe he didn't want to go through all that just so a cop could meet his arrest quota.

- If white people were repeatedly arrested just so cops can meet their arrest quotas, they'd run too.

- He ran like he feared the police might kill him anyway, or plant something on him, as many do. How sad. What has this country become that black people don't trust the police?

He Had a Record

- Many white people have records, but they're still up to 6 times less likely to be killed by the police.

- How does him having a record justify killing him?

- Black people are human. Humans make mistakes.

- We've all made mistakes in the past.

- He could've been one of the countless black men the police have planted drugs or guns on to make up their arrest quotas.

- Then he must've paid for his crime in the past, and there was no reason for the cops to execute him.

- A lot of black people have records for things white people get a slap on the wrist for. He could've have been one of them.

He Was in a Gang

- Belonging to a larger, clearly identifiable, group, like punk rockers, goths, and Hell's Angels is a necessary part of human development. Gangs are one of the only groups available to inner-city kids to join.

- There's an organization called Homeboy Industries that helps people in gangs turn their lives around by giving them opportunities they never had. You can donate to it online.

- Gang culture can be stopped by spending less on military weapons for the police, and using that money to invest in better schools, youth clubs, job training, and decent housing for communities of color.

- Many gang members are forced to join when they're children.

- The people in gangs usually come from America's ghettos. Ghettos are a part of America's systematic racism. Stop racism, stop gang culture.

Black People Wouldn't Be in Jail If They Didn't Commit Crimes

- There's something called the Innocence Project that exonerates people in jail for crimes they didn't commit. Most of them are black.

- Police officers have been fired for planting evidence on innocent black people. For instance, more than 1000 Black men in Alabama were falsely accused and criminalized by a group of racist police officers who planted drugs and guns on them.

- In most states, cops are under orders to make up their arrest quotas in black neighborhoods, so they arrest black people for things like not being able to afford to pay fines for overgrown lawns.

- Actually, many innocent black people plead guilty to get less time for crimes they didn't commit.

- In places like Lexington, Mississippi, there are no state rules governing how long a person can be incarcerated without being formally charged with a crime.

- As of 2002 (the last time the government collected this data nationally), about 29% of people in local jails were unconvicted – that is, locked up while awaiting trial or another hearing. Nearly 7 in 10 (69%) of these detainees were black people.

Rap Music is Violent and Degrades Black Women

- Not all. There's some rap songs about the need to uplift each other, love, racism, and police brutality.

- For centuries, black men were stereotyped as violent and the women as loose, I'm not surprised that's how many see themselves. Most humans are a product of their society.

- Clearly, some black people have internalized negative European stereotypes about them.

- True. I wish record company executives wouldn't sign those artists and radio stations wouldn't play them.

- I bet if white rappers degraded themselves and white women like that, they'd never get signed by record companies or airplay. Racism is insidious.

- It seems Europeans aren't the only people who'll do anything for money.

- Poor people will do anything for money, and record companies are happy to cash in. Black owned record companies need to do better too if they're also putting that stuff out.

- People often see themselves how their society sees them. It's a societal-fulfilling prophecy.

Black People Are a Drain on The System

- The billions of dollars America earned from the enslavement of black people's ancestors financed the system.

- Black people are oppressed and disenfranchised by the system. It's the system's fault.

- The racist justice system and the prison slavery industrial complex would be out of business without black people. That's two systems that rely on black people to keep going. I'm sure there's more.

- Health experts have long blamed racism for higher rates of disease among African Americans. Stopping racism will help them stay healthy. Healthy people contribute more to the system.

- If the ancestors of black people had the chance to live the American Dream, instead of being literally forbidden from creating their own wealth, today their descendants would be contributing more to the system.

- Whole towns of white people have sprung up around prisons where black people are mass incarcerated. The white people in those towns would be unemployed without America's criminalization of black people. That's one way black people are helping the system.

-The racist system has already determined it only wants black people to be slaves to it in prison. That's how they're helping the system, and it's greater sacrifice than the rest of us are making.

Black People Contribute Less Taxes

- Black people pay more taxes than the billionaires who own Amazon and Walmart. Do you have a problem with that? Or do you want to collect from the poor first?

- Tax loopholes make it possible for billionaires to pay less taxes than you do, but you prefer to focus on poor black people. Why is that?

- Poor people, regardless of their color, pay more for everything from banking to toilet paper and other staples, because they're not able to buy in bulk.

- Black people, who usually earn less money than white people, due to systematic racism, shouldn't be in the same tax bracket as white people, but they are.

- Several recent studies and investigations show that, for decades racist tax assessors saddled black residents with property tax bills that were too high given the value of their homes, so those black people were paying more taxes than white people would pay for the same property. Don't worry, racism always makes sure black people pay a higher price, in one way or another.

Black People Should Pull Themselves Up by Their Bootstraps

- After chattel slavery, black people pulled themselves up by building some of the most prosperous towns in America, but jealous white rioters destroyed them, again and again.

- Structural, systematic, institutional racism made it all but impossible for black people to collectively pull themselves up.

- When their enslavement was abolished, black men who started their own businesses were often lynched. And sometimes, white people cut off parts of their bodies and took them home as souvenirs.

- Structural, systematic, institutional racism left them without boots.

- Black people were prevented from pulling themselves up by racist white people who refused to hire them, mass incarcerated them, and poorly educated them after burning down their schools. Even the CIA helped hold them back by dumping drugs in the ghettos black people are still interred in.

- That's easy for a white person to say, since Europeans received a lot more from the government to pull themselves up than black people ever got. One example is the GI Bill that aimed to help American WWII vets by providing them with benefits including low-cost mortgages, low-interest loans, and financial support. Most black vets didn't benefit from the bill due to racism.

Black People Are Only Good at Sports

- Black people might excel at sports due to their good, strong, human genes.

- Black people are good at other things too, including anything a white person can do, given the opportunity.

- There are great black doctors, like Daniel Hale Williams who performed the first successful heart surgery. Black people are good at a lot of things.

- There are great black mathematicians, like Katherine Johnson, who helped send the first American man to the moon. Black people are good at a lot of things.

- There are great black inventers, like Henry T. Sampson, who invented the first cell phone, and others. Black people are good at a lot of things.

Black People Are Ignorant

- Black people invented the modern traffic light, the home security system, gas masks, refrigerated trucks, the bicycle, the hairbrush, the typewriter, the lawn mower, the rotary engine, math, medicine, mining, cooking, architecture, cell phones, calendars, and countless other things. Nothing ignorant about that.

- The first university was built in Africa by a black woman. Do you think she was stupid?

- The Moors, and other groups of Africans, taught Europeans how to bathe and brush their teeth, change their cloths according to the season, how to make paper, and how to read and write, among other things. Can you imagine how ignorant Europeans were before black people educated them?

- Black people brought Europe out of the dark ages by sharing their knowledge with them. I guess some people were born to help others, and some were born to oppress others.

Black People All Look Alike

- If you can't tell the difference between President Obama and Martin Luther King, or Oprah Winfrey and Diana Ross, you should have your eyes checked or fire your eye doctor.

- Everyone is unique. Nature doesn't make copies.

- Really? I can tell them apart. Some are short, some are tall. Some are slim; some are overweight. Some are darker skinned; some lighter skinned. Some have small noses; some have large noses. Some have full lips; some have thinner lips. Does bad vision run in your family?

- There's so much physical diversity in black people, in fact, since all humans come from Africa, we prove how diverse they are.

Black People Look Like/Are Monkeys

- The chimpanzee is our closest relative in nature. Some have white skin, others have black.

- One of the differences between humans and monkeys is humans have lips. A lot of white people don't.

- Humans and monkeys are both primates, but humans are not descended from monkeys or any primate living today.

- All humans share a common ape ancestor with chimpanzees, but it lived between 8 and 6 million years ago. There are none alive today.

- All humans share about 99% of our DNA with chimpanzees, making it our closest living relative. We all share physical similarities with them.

- The pig, who has pink skin, is genetically close to humans. I would rather to look like a monkey than a pig because monkeys at least resemble humans.

- If you can't tell the difference between a human and a monkey, you need a good eye doctor.

Black People Are Ugly

- They say beauty's in the eye of the beholder. In other words, ugly sees ugly, beauty sees beauty.

- 2019, black women were crowned Miss Universe, Miss World, Miss USA, and Miss Teen USA. Ugly people don't win those titles.

- Your opinion of how black people look is only your opinion. I've seen some gorgeous black people in my day.

- You should've told that too all the white people who died of skin cancer for trying to get as black as they could.

- Then why are black countries the number 1 destination for white sex tourists?

Black People Are Lazy

- Forcing other people to work to build your country then refusing to let them live the American dream, that's lazy and cruel.

- When white racists don't employ them, or the only jobs available go to white people, black people are called lazy.

- A 2019 study showed even the country's most highly educated black people are less likely to be employed than their white counterparts. Black people aren't lazy. They're just not getting jobs due to racism.

- Racism is the reason black people find it harder to get a job, not their laziness.

Black People Breed Like Roaches

- White people make up 62% of the population while black people only make up 13%.

- Do you say that about white people who have a lot of children?

- The largest family in America are a white family called the Bates. They have 19 children.

- The two largest families in America are the Bates and the Duggars. They're both white.

I Hate Black People

- A wise person once said, 'all hate starts as self-hate', because people who love themselves don't have it in them to hate others.

- Do you like things like cell phones, elevators, and home security systems, because black people invented them.

- Do you like Rock and Roll, Punk Rock, Country music, jazz, blues, or any modern music genre, because without black people none of that music would exist.

- No point in hating something you can't do anything about.

- Hating other people because they won't change for you leads to unhappiness. Try focusing on personal development, like learning to accept yourself and others as they are. You'll be a lot happier.

- What's the point of hating something that's none of your business?

- Don't tell them that. Black people think all white people love them.

- A hate filled life is a wretched existence. My heart goes out to you.

'Those People' Or 'Niggers'

- I'm thankful white people aren't grouped in together, or I'd die of shame over the horrible things white people have done, and continue to do, to black people.

- Does it make you feel better about yourself to put other people down?

- Putting other people down stems from low self-esteem.

- If all the people who share the same genes are alike, then white people are alike, which worries me. I don't want to be associated with the myth of white supremacy.

- Being seen as an individual is a white privilege.

If Black People Don't Like It, They Should Go Back to Africa

- If they don't like what? Racism. Why should they enjoy being treated as second class citizens in the country their ancestors built?

- Africa is no more their home then Europe is your home.

- Deporting all those people would cost a fortune. It'd be much more cost effective to send you back to Europe.

- If you don't like them, it'd be easier for you to go back to Europe. But black people are there too. Maybe you should accept something you can't do anything about.

- The ancestors of black Americans were here before most Europeans got here.

- Black people have as much right to be in America as white people.

- Africans were here before Europeans arrived. They just didn't steal it. Columbus noted in his journal that the Native Americans confirmed *'black skinned people had come from the south-east in boats, trading in gold-tipped spears.'*.

Black People Shouldn't Get Reparations Because They Were Not Alive During Slavery

- Nothing short of the effort America put into rebuilding Japan after WWII, which included political, economic, and social reforms, will suffice to atone for America's 400+ years' war on black people.

- After chattel slavery supposedly ended, white Americans created Jim Crow laws. One of the purposes of those laws was put black people in prison so they could continue doing slave labor. The practice continues to this day with the war on drugs that mass incarcerates black people, although white people do drugs too.

- Black people were enslaved in the south until the 1960's because many were never told they were free.

- Slavery didn't end when it was supposedly abolished. It continued with the prison industrial complex, that gives black people more time behind bars than white people. They work for pennies in jail. The pay is just a gesture. They're enslaved.

- Reparations are owed to black people for the terror, disenfranchisement, and oppression they've endured since chattel slavery ended.

- Reparations aren't just for slavery, but also for the oppression and racism that continues to this day.

- Slavery in prison continues with the schools to prison pipeline. Schools send black students into the pipeline through zero-tolerance disciplinary policies, which involve the police in minor misbehavior and often lead to arrests and juvenile detention referrals. This causes them to miss school and make friends with criminals. What could possibly go wrong?

Who's Going to Pay for Reparations?

- We can start with the corps worth billions today that got rich out of slavery like Lehman Brother, Aetna Inc, JP Morgan Chase, New York Life, USA Today, and Bank of America, just to name a few.

- Record companies that are worth billions today, made their money ripping off black artists. They should contribute towards black reparations.

- Every year, the Federal Government makes improper payments costing taxpayers $70 billion. Just half of that could go towards reparations every year, saving taxpayers 35 billion.

- The same way America pays for endless wars that no one never questions the cost of.

White People Were Slaves Too

- Irish people were indentured servants who did unpaid labor for a contracted period, then were freed when that time was up.

- Black people were enslaved their entire lives with no possibility of ever being free. They were enslaved, not indentured servants, like Irish people.

- That's a lie to make black people think slavery had nothing to do with racism. The Irish were indentured servants who were eventually freed. Black people were enslaved and never freed until abolition, then they were mass incarcerated to continue being slaves in prison.

- I find it odd there's no films, documentaries, or TV series about the White Slaves of America, don't you?

All Lives Matter

- Then why do you have a problem with black lives mattering?

- If that's true, why are black people still waiting for reparations for slavery, and the horrific racism that followed, which continues to this day?

- People started saying 'Black Lives Matter' because, according to Harvard University, black people are up to 6 times more likely to be killed than white people when stopped by the cops.

- If all lives were at risk when anyone is stopped by the cops, saying 'All Lives Matter' would make sense.

- Not until black lives matter too.

- It seems a lot of people get off on violence, and don't want it to stop towards black people. It's sick.

- If that's true why is there so much racism in America?

Blue Lives Matter

- Tell that to white people, since they kill more cops than black people.

- Only when they're serving and protecting all Americans.

- True, but cops shouldn't be allowed to bully or murder black people.

- No one said cop's lives don't matter.

- If the cops stopped waging war on black people, you wouldn't have to choose a side.

- Cops sometimes die in the line of duty. Being killed for being black shouldn't be consider dying in the line of duty to blackness.

- All lives matter, including black lives.

- Being a cop is sometimes a dangerous job. They know that. Being black shouldn't be considered a dangerous job when they're stopped by the cops.

Cops Kill More White People Than Black People

- White people make up 62% of the population while black people make up only 13%, so any data that doesn't take demographics into account is inaccurate and misleading.

- Per capita, or according to the percentage of the population, cops kill more black people. For example, if 500 white people out of a 3 million die and 450 black people out of 1 million die, a higher percentage of black people are dying.

- That's because there are more white people in America, still, a Harvard University study found black people are up to 6 times more likely to be killed by the police.

Black Lives Matter Was Started by / is Owned by / is Controlled by George Soros

- BLM was started in response to the death of Travon Martin, and the acquittal of his killer, by activists Alicia Garza, Patrisse Cullors, and Opal Tometi. All black women.

- Three black women started BLM, not George Soros.

- George Soros is one of the many people and organizations who donated money to BLM.

- It's sad when a white person gets the credit for something good black people create.

- George Soros donated money to BLM. Since when does donating money mean buying the whole organization? Do I own my local charity shop?

Black Lives Matter Is A Terrorist Organization

- Terrorists are people who use violence and intimidation in pursuit of political aims. You're confusing BLM with the KKK.

- There's a big difference between BLM, who want justice and an end to police brutality, and ISIS, who kill innocent people.

- BLM is trying to stop the police from terrorizing black people the same way police terrorized black people in South Africa.

- BLM never lynched white people, ran white people off their own property, or burned crosses on white people's lawns like the KKK have. I wonder why the KKK are not called a terrorist organization.

Black Lives Matter Is Trying to Start A Race War

- Wrong. America has waged a one-sided, 400-year, war on black people, and BLM have had enough.

- No. BLM are trying to stop the one-sided race war cops, and white America, have been waging on black people for 400 years.

- Racism is a war on black people that robs them of their human rights and dignity. The war is entirely one-sided.

- Slavery, Jim Crow Laws that made being black illegal, lynching's, police brutality, and interring black people in ghettos, prove there's a war being waged on black people. Not the other way around.

- Funny, that's what people were brainwashed to think about the Black Panthers, and all they were trying to do was defend themselves against white racism and police brutality too.

Black Lives Matter is Anti-Police

- No. They're anti the police who kill black people as if they're judge and jury.

- They're anti-police brutality. Big difference.

- White people would also be anti-police if the cops made up their arrest quotas in white neighborhoods and arrested them for things like trespassing at our jobs, like they did many times to a black man named Earl Sampson in Florida.

- The police have gotten away with killing too many innocent black people in America, including women and children, just like the police in South Africa. I don't blame BLM.

- They're anti the fact that black people are up to 6 times more likely to be killed by the police. This stat was confirmed by a Harvard University study.

Being A Cop Is A Hard Job That's Full of Danger

- Does that danger include having to shoot an unarmed black person who's running away in the back?

- The cops sometimes kill black people when their lives clearly aren't in danger. That's the problem.

- The officers who beat Rodney King weren't in danger since he was on all fours as their blows rained down on him.

- That's no excuse for killing sweet, innocent, Elijah McClain. RIP.

- People who don't care when the police kill a black person are the same kind of people who didn't care when a black person was lynched.

- The issue isn't about how dangerous being a cop is. That comes with the territory. It's about cops using excessive force when they're not in any danger.

- This isn't about how dangerous being a cop is, it's about how dangerous being black is when stopped by the cops.

- If they can't take the pressure they should resign.

- That's no excuse for killing someone for something like selling CD's, like those two cops who killed Anton Sterling in Louisiana, and there's countless other cases like that.

The Police Are Not All Bad, There's Just A Few Bad Apples

- A few bad apples spoil the whole the bunch if they're not removed.

- Rotten apples are no more palatable than rotten cops.

- Would you buy a bag of apples knowing some were rotten?

- If a rotten apple killed a member of your family just because they were white, I'm sure you would have a problem with that apple.

- If a bad doctor killed one of your relatives, would you defend her because all doctors aren't bad?

- People who are bad at their jobs are fired. Why should the police be any different?

Defunding the Police Is A Bad Idea

- Defunding doesn't mean abolishing. It means too much money is spent on criminalizing people, while not enough is spent on making sure they have everything they need to reach their full potential.

- Defunding and abolishing are two different things. Although communities of color should be allowed to police themselves, since so many racists are cops.

- The police don't need expensive military weapons because they're not in the army. We should be spending less on the army too.

- If spending so much money on militarizing the police worked there would be less crime.

- Investing more money in good schools, decent housing, daycare, and job training are proven ways to reduce crime. That's what defunding the police means.

- Spending money on military weapons is not a long-term solution to stop crime. Investing that money in communities is proven to stop crime.

I Support the Protests, But I Don't Agree
With the Destruction of Property and Looting

- There are pictures online of white people looting and videos of black people begging them to stop. Have you seen them?

- Historically, Europeans are the world's greatest looters.

- Buildings can be rebuilt. Dead black bodies can't.

- Black lives matter more than property, to me.

- If America cared as much about black lives as it does about property, black people wouldn't have to protest.

- I don't agree with America's 400-year campaign to destroy black lives through racism and police brutality.

- When Colon Kaepernick protested, there was no looting. Maybe the two aren't linked.

- The police have arrested white extremists for starting riots to discredit the BLM movement.

Black People Are Protesting the Wrong Way

- White people with hearts are protesting too.

- When black people peacefully took a knee, that was the wrong way too.

- No matter how black people protest, some white people think it's wrong. It's as if they want racism to continue.

- No one on earth has more patience than black people. They've been peacefully fighting for their human rights for hundreds of years.

- Black people have tried everything except burning the country to the ground. Is that what you suggest?

Taking Down Confederate Monuments Is Wrong

- There's no statues of Hitler in Germany because the Germans aren't proud of what Hitler he did. What part of slavery, rape, and working people to death in concentrations camps, politely called plantations, are you proud of?

- If someone fought for the enslavement your ancestors, which included raping them, selling their children, and working them to death, would you like to see a statue honoring them?

- Only a society of heartless savages erects statues of psychopaths.

- There's really no good reason to have statues of torturers and rapists unless America looks up to people like that.

- What's the point of having statues of losers?

CHAPTER 2
ASIAN PEOPLE

As of July 2nd, 2020, 2,120 anti-Asian American hate incidents related to Covid-19 were reported in the US, and many more went unreported. Those crimes were committed after Trump called Covid-19, *'the Chinese virus'*, to deflect from his abysmal handling of the pandemic. The following statements prove what happens when a responsible adult isn't in charge. Age-old stereotypes about Asian-Americans are also included and debunked.

They're Bringing That Chinese Virus Over Here

- By 'they' do you mean all of them, including the Chinese Americans who've never been to China?

- The first known case of Covid-19 was traced to a Chinese tourist, but once the virus spread all over the world, anyone could have brought it here, causing it to spread, because Trump was so slow to act.

- After Covid-19 spread around the world, Trump took too long to put all travelers in quarantine.

- Although the first known case of Covid-19 was traced to a Chinese tourist, that doesn't mean all Chinese Americans are responsible.

- That's the same as saying, *since white men are the worlds #1 child sex tourists, all white men should be labeled pedophiles.*

They Can Take Their Disease That's Ruining Our Country and Go Back Home

- Chinese American's are just as American as anyone else. This is their home too.

- Chinese people helped build America. Many were here before a lot of Europeans got here.

- China isn't the home of Chinese Americans any more than Europe is the home of European Americans.

- Did you sleep through biology 101? Viruses can't be put back in the bottle and returned to their point of origin.

- Once out, only a competent politician can stop a virus from spreading.

- The country is in ruins because the President, and some Republican politicians, played down the potential harm from the epidemic, which left America vulnerable.

- Personally, I blame the politicians on both sides of the aisle, who, weeks before the pandemic ruined America, sold hundreds of thousands of dollars in stock after attending sensitive, closed door briefings about the threat of the disease. If they also warned Americans about what was to come, lives would have been saved, and the virus would have had a lot less impact.

The Virus Is Their Fault

- This isn't the fault of Chinese Americans. Many have never been to China.

- It's the fault of incompetent politicians like Trump who took too long to respond appropriately to the pandemic.

- People from European countries were still allowed to travel here after the virus hit Europe.

- No one's at fault for a virus that spreads around the world. That's what viruses do.

- So, since it started in China, you blame all Chinese Americans? Wow.

Americans Just Want to Be Safe

- Everyone wants to be safe, including Chinese Americans who helped build this country.

- Then maybe next time Americans should elect a president who knows how to handle a crisis, not one who blames everyone else for his incompetence.

- All Americans deserve to be safe, including Chinese Americans.

- Do you think Chinese Americans don't want to be safe too?

Chinese People Are Good at Math and Science

- Chinese people are good at anything they put their mind too, just like everyone else.

- Chinese people are also good at art, theater, music, acting, sports, and everything else other humans are good at.

- There are some Chinese people who hate math and science, just like everyone else.

- Most people are good at the things their parents encourage and steer them towards at a young age. Math and science are held in high esteem in a lot of Chinses households, and so it should be. Better than encouraging watching TV, being a racist, and drinking beer.

- Other people are good at math and science too.

Chinese People Look Alike

- All humans who share the same gene pool have physical similarities, but nature doesn't make copies. All humans are unique.

- Like all people who share the same gene pool, Chinese people share certain physical traits, but there is variety among all people. Some are short, some are tall. Some are slim, some are overweight. Some are darker skinned, some lighter skinned. Some have small noses; some have large noses. Some have full lips; some have thin lips. Just like all people.

- That's because you are looking for similarities, not differences. They have different eye shapes, face shapes, body types, hair styles, and hair color.

- It's easy for me to tell them apart. Maybe you should have your eyes checked or fire your eye doctor.

CHAPTER 3
JEWISH PEOPLE

Shamefully, in 2020, 75 years after the Nazis were defeated, Neo-Nazism is on the rise. Although Neo-Nazi's also hate other minorities, gays, and Christians, they perceive 'the Jew' as their cardinal enemy. Surprisingly, instead of being outlawed and jailed for hate speech, they can freely gather, march through towns, and make the following anti-Semitic statements. Some may seem 'innocent', but they're antiquated stereotypes that mask hate, so they must be shut down too.

The Holocaust Is A Myth

- Was Hitler, the death camps, and WWII myths too?

- Were all the people who lost friends and family myths too?

- Then why is Germany paying Jewish People reparations?

- Then why did all those ally soldiers return with horror stories about the death camps? Were they in on it too?

- Wow! Are you saying all the film footage of the death camps is CGI? I had no idea the technology was so advanced back then.

- Yeah. And the Aryan Brotherhood wants equality for all.

Heil Hitler!

- Hitler was a hate filled maniac. What's it about him that you identify with?

- Hitler was a failed artist. Goes to show people should follow their dreams, regardless of how little talent they have.

- Hitler obviously had low self-esteem like, like his followers.

- Hitler lost. That saying is outdated and laughable.

- Hitler wanted to make art, but he sucked at that too.

- Hitler is a dead failure. Honoring dead failures says a lot about a person.

I Hate 'The Jew' / Jews

- Referring to a whole group of people as one person is like saying *'The Neo-Nazi has a small penis and low self-esteem.'*.

- Real men don't look for scapegoats, they adapt to hard times.

- That's because you spend too much time focusing on them instead of developing your unique skill set and thereby succeeding in life.

- It must make you very unhappy to hate something you can't do anything about. Why do that to yourself then blame others?

- A hate filled life is a wretched existence. My heart goes out to you.

The Jews Are Good With Money

- Anyone who's financially literate is good with money.

- It's undeniable that Jews are well-represented in finance and business, but when they were denied the right to do much else, being merchants and financiers were two of the only professions open to them.

- Like everyone, Jewish people are good at other things too.

- Their being good at finance can be attributed to the community's high literacy rates.

- During the 18th century, as many as three-fourths of the Jews in Central and Western Europe were only allowed to be retail peddlers and street bankers (money lenders). Most family businesses are handed down through generations.

- When Jews in Central and Western Europe were limited to retail peddling, hawking, and street banking (money lending), the Christians were forbidden from those occupations by their religion. This gave rise to the myth that Jews were morally deficient, which persists to this day.

The Jews Have All the Money

- There are rich Jews, just as there are rich Africans, Arabs, Mexican, Europeans, Latino's, Italians...

- Really? Before Covid 19, which destroyed the economy, how did non-Jews pay their rent, buy cars, boats, planes, cloths, food, purchase shitty Nazi memorabilia, or afford to drink too much beer?

- I have money and I'm not Jewish.

- If you spent as much time on raising your self-esteem as you do thinking about the money other people have, you might be happier, and richer, since personal development tends to lead to abundance.

- A lot of people are broke or out of work due to the bad economy, including many Jewish people.

The Jews Run the Federal Reserve

- The Federal Reserve is still largely white and male and comprised of non-Jews and Jews. But, according to Forbes, pressure is building for that to change, thankfully. All people should be represented everywhere. That's what equal opportunities is all about.

- Jewish people are overrepresented in banking, because in 18th century Central and Western Europe, they were forbidden from most other professions. One of the few things they could do was street banking (money lending).

- Some of the people on the board of the Federal Reserve are Jewish, but some are not.

- The Board of the Federal Reserve is made up of Jewish and non-Jewish Europeans, I think there should be more Tribespeople, black people, Latino's, and Mexicans, don't you?

- In the banks 105-year history-year history, only one black person has sat on the board. The others were all European or-Jewish. That's more to do with white male supremacy than anything else.

Jews Control the World Banking System

- The international financial institutions like World Bank (IMF) are controlled by USA, UK, France, Japan, and Germany.

CHAPTER 4
LGBTQ PEOPLE

Religious fanatics, the closeted, and people who cannot mind their own business, have one thing in common: a hatred of LGBTQ people. The fanatics believe the bible is the word of God, including 9 mentions of unicorns He forgot to create. The closeted don't need to be reminded of their desires. The busybodies lead such dull lives that they're forced to obsess about what others do with their genitalia. Whatever their reason for not minding their own business, the hate, judgment, and ignorance evident in the following statements demand informed replies.

God Hates LGBTQ people

- I don't live my life by the bible. Lot's daughters got him drunk then had sex with him. Genesis 19:30-38.

- God must also hate Unicorns, since they're mentioned in the bible, but he decided to not create them.

- Or maybe God created gays to help keep the population down? There's enough humans on earth as it is.

- The bible was written by men, not God, and even Catholic priests don't believe a word of it.

- If Catholic priests don't believe a word of the bible, why should I?

Being Gay Goes Against Nature

- Some same sex birds do it. So do beetles, sheep, fruit bats, dolphins, and orangutans. All those animals are a part of nature.

- Are animals a part of nature? Because homosexual and bisexual activity is not unknown within the animal kingdom.

HIV And AIDS Was God's Curse on Gays

- AIDS has killed, and continues to kill, heterosexuals too. It seems your 'all loving' God has cursed everyone. I wonder if He'll repent. Like Genesis 6:6 says He does.

Lesbians Hate Men

- Just because lesbians aren't sexually attracted to men doesn't mean they hate men.

- Most people aren't sexually attracted to goats. That doesn't mean they hate goats.

- A lot of straight women say they're gay when they don't find a man attractive and want to get rid of him. Has that ever happened to you?

- Most lesbians have relationships with men who are family members, friends, or colleagues. Do you think they secretly hate them, but are afraid to come out with it?

LGBTQ People Sleep Around A Lot

- Being LGBTQ doesn't make a person sexually promiscuous. That's just a heterosexual fantasy.

- Not all. That's the same as saying, *heterosexual people don't sleep around.*

- LGBTQ people are as capable of long-term, monogamous, relationships as heterosexuals are.

Trans People Are Mentally Ill

- Both the American Medical Association and the American Psychiatric Association don't consider being transgender a mental disorder. Do you know better? What qualifications do you hold?

- Although it's true LGBTQ people suffer from anxiety and depression, that has more to do with them being demonized and attacked physically for being who they are then anything else. Straight people also suffer from anxiety and depression.

Trans Women Are Men

- They are people who were born with male genitalia but identify as women. Men don't identify as women.

- They may seem like men to those who obsessively focus on the genitalia of others, but they identify as women, and it's really not our business, is it?

- I think people should be allowed to be who are. It has nothing to do with me.

- Men who wear woman's clothing but identify as men are drag queens. Trans people are born with male genitalia but identify as women, so they wear women's clothing. And they're free to do so.

Trans Men Are Women

- They are people who were born with female genitalia but identify as men. Women don't identify as men.

- They many seem like women to those who obsessively focus on the genitalia of others, but they identify as men, and it's really not our business, is it?

- I think people should be allowed to be who are. It has nothing to do with me.

- Women who wear men's clothing but identify as women just like wearing men's clothing. Trans men are born with female genitalia but identify as men, so they wear men's clothing. And they're free to do so.

Gay Men Are Sexual Predators and Pedophiles

- Gay men only account for 1% of the cases in which children were molested by an adult male.

- Then why is the white heterosexual male the worlds #1 child sex tourist?

- Then why are girls the number #1 victims of child rape in the world?

- According to the American Psychological Association, children aren't more likely to be molested by gay men than they are by heterosexual men.

- A University of California study found no evidence that gay men molest children at higher rates than straight men, in fact, just the opposite.

- That's based on the erroneous idea that men who molest male children must be gay, but according to research, there's two types of child molesters, fixated and regressive. The fixated type is not considered gay or straight because he usually finds adults of either sex to be repulsive. The regressive type is usually attracted to other adults and are in heterosexual relationships.

Gay People Are Trying to Convert Everyone

- No one can become gay. If they can be easily swayed, then they're either bi or closeted.

- Then why do they use gay hook up apps instead of straight dating apps?

- Some straight people try to convert gay people, some succeed, some don't, same applies to some gay people.

- Does that mean being straight is a choice, for you?

- That's silly. They exist due to straight people.

- No one can become gay. If they can be easily swayed, then they're either bi or closeted.

Same Sex Parents Harm Children

- The American Academy of Pediatrics has determined that children with gay or lesbian parents are as healthy emotionally, cognitively, and socially as children with heterosexual parents. I'll take their word for it.

- No credible study has found that same-sex parents are more harmful than heterosexual parents.

- In 2013, The American Academy of Child and Adolescent Psychiatry found that children with same sex parents are no more likely to develop emotional or behavioral problems than children with heterosexual parents.

- The Child Welfare League of America's official position is: Lesbian, gay, and bisexual parents are as well suited to raise children as heterosexual parents.

Gay People Were Sexually Abused as Children

- Then why are the vast majority of people who were sexually abused heterosexual?

- No credible study has found a link between sexual orientation and childhood sexual abuse.

- There are significantly more cases of child sexual abuse than there are people who identify as LGBTQ. The numbers don't add up.

- The statistics agree that female children are more likely to be sexually abused than males, but there's a lot more gay men than there are lesbian. How's that?

Gay People Shouldn't Be Allowed to Serve in The Army

- Gay people have been serving in the army since the invention of armies.

- Openly gay people have served in 25 countries, including Britain, Israel, South Africa, Canada, and Australia.

- In countries like Britain, Israel, South Africa, Canada, and Australia, where gay people serve openly, there's been no negative impact on recruitment numbers, length of duty, morale, readiness, or overall combat effectiveness.

Gay People Are More Likely to Abuse Drugs and Alcohol

- Yeah, and heterosexuals are not likely to abuse drugs and alcohol.

- Really? I wonder why? You'd think they live in a society that hates them or something.

- OMG! Do you suppose all those heterosexuals who've been to AA were faking?

- Studies have determined that many LGBTQ people turn to drugs and alcohol due to the stress of being in an often-hostile society, but straight people don't have that excuse and they turn to drugs and alcohol too.

- That has more to do with them having to share a planet with people who can't mind their own business, think every word in the bible is true, including 9 mentions of unicorns, or are envious of their openly gay lifestyle.

Being Gay Is a Choice

- Why would anyone choose to be something religious fanatics who believe in unicorns, people who can't mind their own business, and repressed gay people have such a big problem with?

- Is being straight a choice, for you?

- How would you know? Have you decided to be straight?

- Gay conversion therapy has been found to be a hoax invented by unhinged religious fanatics, many of whom eventually come out as being gay themselves.

- The American Psychological Association has concluded that instances of people going from gay to straight are rare, and individuals who claimed to have been 'converted' often continue to experience same sex attractions.

No One Is Born Gay

- The American Psychological Association concludes 'Most people experience little or no choice about their sexual orientation.'

- In 1994, the American Psychological Association noted that 'homosexuality is not a matter of individual choice' and that research 'suggests that homosexual, (as well as heterosexual), orientation is in place very early in the life cycle, possibly before birth.'

- No one is born nosy.

- No one is born believing in unicorns, but they're in the bible.

- No one should have to repress what they are due to a book that mentions unicorns 9 times.

CHAPTER 5
MEXICAN PEOPLE

For centuries, Mexican people have experienced some form of racism in America. But now, due to the racist comments Trump makes about them, hate speech targeting Mexican People has become a national pastime. The statements that follow are perfect examples of the bottomless pit of ignorance that signifies what it means to be a Trump supporter. The replies will help teach them how valuable Mexicans are to American society, and the question, *who was here first?* is answered to.

Mexican 'Illegals' Are Murderers and Thieves

- The typical Mexican 'illegal' is an honest, hardworking person who's here trying to create a better life for his/her family.

- There's more stories in the press about white people stealing and murdering than Mexican 'illegals'.

- Why do they bother to work so hard if they're stealing?

- With all the hours they work, where do they find the time to murder and steal? Their lunch breaks.

- No one in history has murdered more people or stolen more from others than Europeans.

Mexican 'Illegals' Don't Pay Taxes

- Mexican 'illegals' pay sales taxes and payroll taxes but never file tax returns out of fear of being deported. That provides the government with billions in revenue that's never claimed back.

- The people who employ Mexicans illegally pay them less, so they earn more money, resulting in them paying more taxes to the US and State Treasuries.

- Mexican 'illegals' pay sales taxes and payroll taxes when they buy things or work anywhere.

Mexican 'Illegals' Are on Welfare Getting Unearned Benefits

- No one can apply for welfare without a social security number.

- Mexican 'illegals' live in fear of being deported, so they rarely seek social services.

- The only social services 'illegal' Mexicans risk being deported over are emergency care and primary education, but they contribute a lot more due to all the unclaimed employee taxes they pay.

- No. You need a social security number to get welfare, like the majority of white people on welfare.

- No. You need a social security number to get welfare, like the majority of white people on welfare.

Mexican 'Illegals' Are Stealing All the Jobs

- Mexicans 'illegals' are here doing the jobs American's consider too unpleasant, unsanitary, or unsafe to be worth the wages.

- Mexicans 'illegals' are doing jobs Americans don't want to do. That's not stealing. That's picking up the slack.

- Many illegal employers know their workers are illegal, but they hire them anyway so they can pay them slave wages.

- The people who employ Mexican 'illegals' so they can pay them less are the ones denying Americans jobs.

- Mexican migrant laborers have been working in America since the 1890's and are still doing the same jobs. When exactly did they steal your job?

Mexicans Are Coming Here Illegally

- The Mexicans were here before the Europeans got here, or it wouldn't have been possible for Europeans to steal Texas and California from them.

- According to the people who had this country stolen from them, European colonizers and their descendants are here illegally too. But I guess that doesn't matter due to white privilege.

- The Europeans, who came here illegally, didn't go through immigration. It was only after they stole this country that they made up rules about borders.

- No one is on Earth illegally, that's another European myth.

- Immigration laws are a European invention that didn't apply to Europeans when they first came here.

Mexican 'Illegals' Contribute Nothing to Our Society

- The Southwest and California were built my mostly undocumented Mexican immigrants.

- The California Gold Rush, which started months after America stole California from Mexico, produced hundreds of millions of dollars (billions in today's dollars) for America.

- Mexican mule trains were used to deliver much needed supplies to mining camps and towns throughout the California's Sierra Nevada mountains.

- Mexican 'illegals' pay more taxes that billionaires, and they never claim them back.

- So, doing the jobs Americans consider to be too unpleasant, unsanitary, or unsafe to be worth the wages means 'contributing nothing' to you?

CHAPTER 6
MUSLIM PEOPLE

Islamophobia, exaggerated fear, hatred, and hostility towards Islam and Muslims, is caused by the negative stereotypes created by media coverage that gives the impression that Muslim terrorism is more prevalent than it is. Although white American males commit the most acts of terror on American soil, the following statements prove many Americans aren't aware who the real terrorists are. The replies will help educate them while revealing the truth about Muslim-Americans and Islam.

Islam Is A Religion That Promotes Violence and Terrorism

- There is no text in the Qur'an that endorses terrorism or violence against innocents.

- Then why do American-Muslim leaders and organizations repeatedly denounce violence?

- Islam totally prohibits violence against the innocent and terrorism.

- Islam prohibits terrorism and violence against the innocent. Meanwhile, America is the most violent country on Earth, and white men, not Muslims, commit the most terrorist acts in the USA.

- America's wars for the Earth's resources, that kill millions of innocent people, promotes violence and terrorism.

Muslims Are Terrorists

- White men have committed more acts of terrorism in America than Muslims.

- Since 9/11, the Muslim-American community has helped security and law enforcement officials prevent two of every five al Qaeda terrorist plots against the United States.

- Tips from the Muslim-American community are the largest single source of initial information to authorities about al Qaeda plots against the US. I wish white people would do the same about white male terrorism.

- Yet American-Muslim leaders and organizations repeatedly denounce violence.

Islam Teaches Followers to Oppress Women

- Historically, Islam promoted woman's rights.

- The Qur'an grants women freedom they didn't have before, such as the right to inherit property, conduct business, and have access to knowledge. Long before American women had that right.

- Arranged marriages are more of a cultural than religious practice, and women have the right to divorce.

- The oppression many women face in Muslim countries is caused by cultural tradition, not Islamic law.

Muslim Women Are Forced by Men to Wear
A Headscarf, Or Hijab, As A Sign of Submission

- Islamic law says the Hijab is to protect a woman's modesty, not suppress her.

- It depends upon the country. Muslim women in Saudi Arabia must cover everything but their eyes, hands, and feet, while Muslim women in Turkey observe no special rules about dress.

- Women in other religions also wear special clothing, such as Amish women, Catholic nuns, some Mormons, and Orthodox Jewish women.

Muslims Want to Make Us Live Under Sharia Law

- American-Muslim voting patterns show they're Democrats, Republicans, Progressives, Libertarians, liberals, and conservatives. That doesn't seem like a unified effort to make everyone live under Sharia Law.

- I think the Muslims who have been here for 400 years are happy with the laws of the land, don't you?

- There is no one political platform of Muslims in the US. They're doctors and scientists who are smart enough to know laws can't be changed without a political platform.

Muslims Hate America

- You only think that because 80% of media coverage of Islam and Muslims is negative, but Muslim Americans have contributed a lot of good to American society since coming here on slave ships.

- Does their hate involve being members of the Boys and Girls scouts, Elks Lodges, and American veterans of foreign wars?

- I guess they're showing their hate by being members of school boards and volunteering in community centers.

- Then why did Muslims open free health clinics for poor Americans in Chicago's Southwest side and Los Angeles?

- Approximately 50,000 Muslim Americans are physicians. That's a weird terrorist cell, don't you think?

- Shaquille O'Neal, Kareem Abdul-Jabbar, Michael Jordan, and Mike Tyson are Muslims. How much do you think they hate America?

Muslims want to Destroy America

- The history of Muslims in America goes back 400 years. What's taking them so long?

- The first documented arrival of Muslims to America was on slave ships in the 17th century. Enslaved Africans built America and created all of its wealth. They didn't destroy it.

- Most Muslims who migrate to America do so for the same reasons everyone else does, for economic opportunity and freedom from oppression.

- I guess Muslims like Shaquille O'Neal, Kareem Abdul-Jabbar, Michael Jordan, and Mike Tyson are doing their best to destroy America, but are failing.

- Do you think the 50,000 Muslim American physicians have some sort of plan, other than healing sick Americans?

- There's evidence Muslims were on the ships with Christopher Columbus. They don't seem to be in any big hurry.

The Muslim God Is Allah

- Allah is the name Muslims call God. Jews call the same God Yahweh.

- Allah isn't a different God, it's the name Muslims call the same God Jews and Christians follow.

- To Muslims, Allah is the God of Abraham, Moses, Jesus, and Mary.

CHAPTER 7
TRIBESPEOPLE

According to Hollywood, the original inhabitants of Turtle Island (America) were all killed. According to mainstream media, they're invisible. According to American sports teams, they only exist as degrading mascots. Yet, despite the greatest genocide in history, in which 100 million Tribespeople perished, they're still here. But, instead of being celebrated for their fortitude and diverse culture, they're the target of hate speech, stereotyped, and mocked at sporting events. The following statements reveal the disrespect such a proud and noble people must endure. The replies will defend their honor and expose who the uncivilized, bloodthirsty savages really were.

They Shouldn't Change the Name/Mascot of My Team

- How would you like it if the people who slaughtered your ancestors and stole your country named their teams after you?

- White sports should have European names like The Colonizers, The Settlers and The Steelers should be spelled correctly.

- The Germans haven't named their teams after the Jewish people they slaughtered. Only psychopaths like to have reminders of the people they killed.

- How would you like it if the people who committed genocide on your ancestors used degrading depictions of them, and you, as their team mascots?

- Why don't they replace them with derogatory mascots of Europeans?

- I think there's something sinister about naming teams after the people Europeans slaughtered and stole this country from.

Those Mascots Honor Native Americans

- They don't like being called 'Native American' any more than they like being 'honored' by comical stereotypes.

- Those mascots are often negative, that's not the way to honor them.

- Those 'honorable' mascots remind Tribespeople of the ugly, demeaning, stereotypes people have of them.

- Seeing themselves as comical, unattractive, stereotypes adversely effects how they see themselves.

- Who would be honored by stereotypes that are an example of prejudice by the dominant culture?

Native Americans Are Drunks

- Europeans introduced them to alcohol because drunk people are easier to take advantage of.

- I guess they drink to forget what the Europeans did to them.

- Anyone who had everything stolen from them by the people they helped would be forgiven for having a drink problem.

- If your way of life was destroyed by the people you welcomed into your house, you might have issues with alcohol too.

- White people are drunks too. And no one stole their country. What's their excuse?

- I bet they have a lot of regrets. Especially helping the settlers get through the winter without starving.

I Thought They Lived in Teepees

- They would be forgiven for thinking Europeans still lived in caves before they left Europe, considering how they treated their hosts.

- No, when Europeans stole their land then murdered their woman and children, they were forced onto reservations where they now live in houses.

- That was a long time ago, and no one wants to be reminded of what Europeans did to them when they lived in teepees.

- They don't anymore, but those teepees took genius to build, and they inspired tents, the best thing that happened to camping since campfires.

They Took Only $24 Dollars for Manhattan

- The Tribespeople had no concept of what buying and selling land was. It takes a sick mind to think it can own something it didn't create. They most likely thought they were being paid for the use of the land.

- They were promised more, but there's no record of the Dutch being true to their word, which was typical of Europeans.

- The Dutch took advantage of them.

- Eventually, they learned to not do deals with bloodthirsty, greedy savages.

We Civilized Those Savages

- Europeans defined the word 'savage' by treating them as if they had no idea how to behave like humans.

- There's nothing civilized about murdering your host, slaughtering their women and children, then stealing their land.

- If they were savages, they wouldn't have helped the settlers get through the winter.

- No, it was the Europeans who went full on savage on them, then stole everything they had.

- If by 'savage' you mean someone who doesn't know how to return kindness, then they weren't the savages.

- What part of 'civilizing' involves teaching them what genocide is?

They Attacked and Killed the Settlers

- The settlers settled on their land. What would you have done?

- Would you have stood by and done nothing after your former guests slaughtered your women and children, then stole your land?

- I bet they wished they killed them on sight, instead of treating them like human guests.

- I'm sure that's what Europeans would have done if anyone went to Europe, slaughtered millions, then stole their land.

CHAPTER 8
RACISM, BIGOTRY,
INTOLERANCE IN DISGUISE

Hate speech fronting as a joke or opinion is no more acceptable than any other kind. The person who writes or says any of the following comments may be regurgitating something they heard on the news, passing racism off as a joke, couching their hate in pride, or projecting what they are onto others. Whatever the case, they always stem from ignorance or hate and must be dealt with effectively.

That's Reverse Racism

- Really? Are white people being lynched, interred in ghettos, mass incarcerated, and paid less for doing the same work as black people?

- If racism is being reversed then white racism is a fact, and they are behind by 400 years. Chill out.

- Black people have endured 400 years of structural, systematic, institutional racism. Now it's being reversed. Wow. Will we wind up slaves?

- Do you really think white people are being treated as horribly as black people have for 400+ years?

- Racism requires the power to destroy a person's life based on an opinion of them. How has your life been destroyed by black racism?

- Are you in the same amount of pain as a black woman who knows she will never see her baby again is because it was sold to another plantation?

- You sound like a member of your family was lynched for being white.

- A study shows black babies are 3 times more likely to die when they are born to white doctors, but there's no mortality risk to white babies born to black doctors. So, there's no reverse racism there.

Black History Month Is Racist Because It Excludes White People

- Without Black History Month, most people would still think black history started with their enslavement and ended with the civil rights movement. Now we're finding out black people contributed so much to society and changed it for the better.

- Black History Month is necessary because even in predominantly black schools the focus has been mainly on the history and achievements of white people.

- What's racist is how black history has been left out of the curriculum for centuries.

- The other 11 months are dedicated to white history or only cover slavery and the Civil Rights movement. Do you have a problem with that?

Black People Say the Word 'Ni**er' Too

- Black people should be applauded for turning a word white people used as an excuse to degrade and kill them into a term of endearment. That's genius. But white people have no right to use it.

- White people didn't use that word the same way in the past as black people use it today.

- Black people have the right to use that word however they choose, but white people don't, because it was used by their ancestors as an excuse to commit hate crimes against black people.

- The meaning of the word changes when a white person uses it due to history.

- Black people have said they don't like it when white people use that word. Why don't you care about their feelings?

The Word 'Cracker' Is as Offensive As The Word 'Nigger

- As far as I know, black people never went out looking for a cracker to lynch.

- How many of your ancestors were denied their human rights because black people thought they were crackers, not humans?

- Really? Did anyone ever tell you to get your cracker ass out of town before sundown?

- Especially after all the racism white people have endured due to being seen as 'crackers', not humans.

I'm Proud to Be an American

- Everyone is proud and happy to an American, unless they are victims of America's racism, bigotry, and intolerance.

- What part of slavery, rape, and working people to death in concentrations camps, or plantations, are you proud of?

- Me too. America is a beautiful, diverse, country.

- I'm proud too, but I'm also ashamed about how Europeans treated tribespeople, the enslaved, and their descendants. It continues to this day. We need to right that wrong.

I'm Proud to Be White

- All colors matter.

- What makes you the proudest. The genocide, the slavery, or the racism?

- Skin color isn't an achievement. Loving your human family in a world full of hate is an achievement.

- Skin color doesn't matter to me as much as a person's character.

- I'm proud to not be a racist in a world of white supremacy.

The White Race Should Stay White

- Humans originated in Africa, so there's African genes in white people, since we all come from Africa.

- The idea that 'white' is a race is a myth that justifies racism.

- White is not a race. There's only one race, human.

- Humans are not laundry. When humans stick to the same gene pool it's called inbreeding, which results in birth defects like retardation, idiocy, dwindling birth numbers, and the need for fertility clinics.

- Having dark skin on a planet with a sun is called 'intelligent design'.

I Can't Help It. That's How I Was Raised

- Do you still believe in Santa Clause and the Tooth Fairy?

- No one has to believe everything they were taught when they were a child, unless they want to.

- There was a time when white people thought black people were not fully human, then they learned all humans come from Africa. Stupid ideas change with facts.

- Where there's a will there's a way.

- Many people spend their adult lives undoing their brainwashing, you can too.

- Bad habits are meant to be broken.

You're A Race Traitor

- There's only one race of humans. Anyone who doesn't accept other humans because of the color of their skin is a race traitor.

- There is only one race. It is called 'human'. How am I a race traitor?

- There is only one race. It is called 'human'. Are you saying I'm a color traitor? All colors matter.

- Everyone who is human is the same race.

- I just don't hate humans who don't look like me, because I know there's only one race of humans.

- No. I've just evolved past the need to identify with a skin color. I'm a soul being human.

Knock, Knock, Who's There? Racism, Bigotry, Or Intolerance

- I don't think that's funny. I think it's hatred, bigotry, or intolerance disguised as a joke.

- Making jokes about whole groups of people is a of sign of low self-esteem.

- I think saying degrading things about other people only highlights our low self-esteem.

- Apparently, people who put other people down, even in jest, do so to make themselves feel superior to them.

- Grouping people together strips them of their individuality. Nature never makes exact copies.

CHAPTER 9
HATE IN DENIAL

The term 'gaslight' originated from the 1938 play of the same name (and 1944 film adaptation). The story is about how the protagonist's husband slowly manipulates her into believing she's going mad. He does this by making her think things that are happening around her are figments of her imagination. People who deny racism, bigotry, or intolerance, by saying or writing any of the following comments, are doing the same thing. The replies could have been written for the character in the play who sees through the husbands attempt to make his wife think she can't trust what her mind knows to be true.

I Don't See Color

- How do you manage to cross the street?

- Really? What color is my hair/nail polish/your shirt...?

- The brain picks up on things even when we don't acknowledge them.

- You're missing some beautiful sunsets.

- Even dogs can see yellow, blue, and violet. You're missing out.

- It's OK to see color. Living in a world where some people are treated better than others because of their color is not OK.

- What you can or cannot see doesn't erase 400 years of structural, systematic, institutional racism.

- I do and I celebrate our differences. Black is beautiful.

Donald Trump Is Not A Racist

- The Justice Department sued Donald Trump's company- TWICE- for not renting apartments to black people. Only a racist does that.

- Trump refused to condemn the white supremist who endorsed him. Only another racist does that.

- Trump condoned the beating of a Black Lives Matter protester. Only a racist does that.

- Trump called all Mexicans murderers and rapists. Only a racist generalizes about people like that.

- Trump Called Colon Kaepernick a 'son of a bitch' for peacefully protesting police brutality. Only a pro police brutality racist would say that.

I Just Want America To Be Great Again

- Yeah, me too, but we have a long way to go before this is a great country for everyone.

- America will never be great until it atones for its crimes against black and brown humanity.

- We owe America's greatness to enslaved black people who created all of Americas wealth, which made it a superpower. White people can now help make it great by ending racism, which is a stain on our nation.

- America became great due to the enslavement, rape, and torture of black people, generating billions of dollars out of their pain and suffering. I hope we never go back to that.

- No country is great until it's great for all its citizens.

I Have A Black Friend

- Murderers have friends who are alive.

- Having a black friend doesn't exempt you from being a racist.

- The founding fathers wrote in the constitution that all men were created equal, but they had slaves.

- That doesn't give you the right to say something that's racist.

- Black people are full of compassion and understanding for others.

I Can't Help It. That's How I Was Raised

- Do you still believe in Santa Clause and the Tooth Fairy?

- No one has to believe everything they were taught when they were a child, unless they want to.

- There was a time when white people thought black people were not fully human, then they learned all humans come from Africa. Stupid ideas change with facts.

- Where there's a will there's a way.

- Many people spend their adult lives undoing their brainwashing, you can too.

- Bad habits are meant to be broken.

Racism Is in The Past Because America Had A Black President

- Donald Trump was elected because there's always a white backlash to black progress.

- '*Make America Great Again*' really means '*put white supremacy back in charge again*'.

- Obama received more death threats than all other presidents combined because he's a black man.

- Obama's election didn't end racism in America. I wish it were that easy.

- No other president in history was as disrespected as Obama. The Republicans said they wouldn't work with him even before he took office. That's the first time a losing party ever said that. It was because Obama's a black man.

Everyone Can Succeed If They Work Hard Enough

- Structural, systematic, institutional racism exists so some people won't succeed.

- True, and it's sad that even black college graduates have a harder time getting a job than a white high school dropout and have less wealth then white high school graduates due to racism.

- Black people have always had to work harder than white people, and many succeed. Bless them.

- Those who succeed, despite an unleveled playing field, are extraordinary humans.

- No one succeeds like someone who doesn't have to overcome structural, systematic, institutional racism.

- Earl Sampson is a black man from Miami Gardens, Florida, who, beginning in 2008, was repeatedly arrested by police for trespassing while he was at his own place of employment. All he was trying to do was succeed.

My Grandfather/Parents Came to America With Nothing

- There would've been nothing for your grandfather/parents to come to if black people didn't turn America into the land of opportunity and wealth with their forced free labor.

- America was built by enslaved black people before your grandfather/parents got here.

- Your grandfather/parents had opportunities in America enslaved black people who created all of its wealth, and their descendants, never had.

- Your grandfather/parents were Europeans, so they were not enslaved, jailed, lynched, and mass incarcerated. That helped.

- Did they arrive on slave ships than have 400 years of racism to overcome?

- Was that before or after enslaved black people built American and made it the land of opportunity for your grandfather/parents?

My Life Has Not Been Easy, And I'm White

- Few people have had an easy life, but the color of your skin hasn't made your life harder.

- Yes, but your life hasn't been harder because you're white.

- OK. But being white has never been a disadvantage.

- Everyone goes through trials and tribulations, but yours weren't due to systematic, institutional racism and oppression.

- How have white people been oppressed for being white in America?

I Don't Have Special Privileges

- Would you fear for your life if you were stopped by the police?

- Have you ever been followed around a store because the security guard thought you were going to steal something?

- If you wanted to move, do you think you could rent or purchase housing in an area you can afford and want to live in?

- Being white in a racist society is a privilege you're not aware of because it's a part of your identity. You can't see it as separate from yourself. Black people can see it as something separate from themselves though.

- Privilege is knowing the Supreme Court never had to decide if you should have the same rights as anyone else.

- You have the privilege of being able to deny racism exists.

ONE MORE THING...

Thank you for reading *How To Be A Good Ally Book 1 500 Ways To Shut Down Hate Speech*. Your desire to help make the world a better place for all by speaking out against hate is truly commendable.

If you wish to discuss something in this book, or join the mailing list and be the first to find out when the next book in this series will be available, write me at goodallybooks@gmail.com. You can also contact me on FB at Good Ally Books.

Also, if you enjoyed this book or found it useful, I would be very grateful if you would post a short review on Amazon. Your support does make a difference. I read all the reviews personally, so I can get your feedback and make future editions of this book even better. If you would like to leave a review, then you can do so via your hardcopy order.

Thank you!

ABOUT THE AUTHOR

Linda Tolbert is a native New Yorker who lived in the UK for twenty-two years, where she worked as a model, singer, and voice-over artist. Linda is an early year's (0-25) developmental specialist, trained in the Montessori Method. She has managed youth clubs, taught in pupil referral units, and facilitated self-esteem workshops with teens. Linda is passionate about fighting for everyone's right to be who they are, consequently, she's also the secret identity of Soul Sista #1, the superhero whose arch enemy is The Bully with a Thousand Faces. To find out more visit soulsista1.net

Printed in Great Britain
by Amazon